T5-CRM-433

WITHDRAWN

WILDA W. MARTIN

Clearing

7-35

Clearing

Poems from a Journey

Dale Zieroth

Anansi/Toronto

269581

PR
9199
Z5
C5

Some of these poems have appeared in or been accepted for:
*Quarry, Impulse, Saturday Night, Copperfield, Far Point,
Queen's Quarterly, Alive, Miss Chatelaine, The Lake Winder-
mere Valley Echo,* and on CBC *Anthology.*

Copyright © Dale Zieroth 1973

Design: Karin Loconte
Photo: Margery Zieroth

Published with the assistance of the Canada Council and the
Ontario Arts Council

Typesetting by Annie Buller Typesetting
Printed in Canada by The Hunter Rose Company

ISBN: Paper 0-88784-029-9 / Cloth 0-88784-130-9
Library of Congress Card Number: 73-85576

House of Anansi Press Limited
35 Britain Street
Toronto, Canada

1 2 3 4 5   77 76 75 74 73

For the people who live with me, wherever they are. For Walt and Dennis and Ann who have helped me with these poems; for Ron and Isabelle who have helped me live here; and for Marge, who has done both.

PRAIRIE GRADE SCHOOL

Even now, we entered quietly, afraid
to interrupt and wondering about the
unlocked door. Later we would speak of
the broken water cooler, covered with dust
and the tracks of mice, of the word
scratched with a nail on the blackboard, of
the smell of damp earth and rot. We had
almost expected this. Still, no one
would mention how we were surprised not so much
by the dead meadowlark in the broken window
as by its silence . . .

In this room, it is easy to remember
the broken legs, the new swear words, the
election of Louis St. Laurent. Here we sat
in rows, memorizing rules that were intended
to last for life; our teachers, young ladies
from Neepawa or bigger towns a great distance away,
always to the south. I was here on the day
things first changed, the day I hid from friends
who learned to play without me, discovering
I controlled nothing and growing afraid
for the first time of ordinary trees . . .

From the distance of less than a mile,
nothing seems changed. The building,
standing at a crossroads (one road
goes nowhere, another the only road
to the last farmer before the bush begins),
still colonizes the half acre of land
seven immigrant fathers and a municipal clerk
stole from the prairie. It remains,
useful only as landmark. And landmark
to none but the homecoming sons of farmers.

1

MANITOBA POEM

In Manitoba, a farmer will prepare
for spring and contrary to popular notion
women are not foremost in men's
minds: the new warmth has made them
aware of trains and hills, of things
that would make them leave women completely:
something else keeps them. And the women
are just as glad for the rest.

Summer comes in from Saskatchewan on
a hot and rolling wind. Faces
burnt and forearms burnt, the men seed
their separate earths and listen to the CBC
for any new report of rain. Each day now
the sun is bigger and from the kitchen
window, it sets a mere hundred feet behind
the barn, where a rainbow once came down.

Four months later this is over, men
are finished. Children return
to school and catch colds in their
open jackets. Women prepare
for long nights under 6-inch goosedown
quilts. Outside, the trees shake off
their leaves as if angered by the new
colours. And without any more warning than
this, winter falls on the world,
taking no one by surprise. No one.

THE HUNTERS OF THE DEER

The ten men will dress in white
to match the snow and leave the last
farmhouse and the last woman, going
north into the country of the deer. It
is from there, and from past there, that
the wind begins that can shake
every window in the house and leaves
the woman wishing she had moved away
five years and five children ago.

During the day the father of her children
will kill from a distance. With the others
he will track and drive each bush
and at least once he will kill before
they stop and come together for
coffee in scratched quart jars. And
sometimes the November sun will glint
on the rifles propped together in the snow.

In the evening, as they skin and gut,
they talk about the one that ran three
miles on a broken leg and the bitch wolf
they should have shot and how John
the bachelor likes eating more than
hunting and they pass the whiskey
around to keep warm. In the house
the woman makes a meal from pork.

These men are hunters and later,
standing in bright electrically lighted
rooms they are embarrassed with the
blood on their clothes and although the
woman nods and seems to understand,

she grows restless with their talk.
She has not heard another woman in fourteen days.

And when they leave, the man sleeps
and his children sleep while the woman
waits and listens for the howling of
wolves. To the north, the grey
she-wolf smells the red snow and howls.
She also is a hunter of the deer.
Tonight, while other hunters sleep, she
drinks at the throat.

GLENELLA, MANITOBA

The village, east of highway five,
huddles by the only railway tracks in
fifty miles. One white grain elevator
tells you where you are, from any
direction. After four fires the place
is still big enough to have the
usual buildings: school, hall,
station, hotel and two stores.
Sunday evenings, a passenger
train; Thursday, a freight.
There are no factories here
and no luxuries. On two sides
there are hay fields and country;
machinery and men sometimes move
there. North of here is nothing.

On Saturday night there are Indians
sick in the pub and Crazy John sitting
in the poolhall where he's sat for years
watching the spinning balls, the young men,
who knows what. Visitors soon discover
there are some here who like
what they have lived through. Mostly, there
are young men who stand waiting
with their hands made fists in
pockets that are empty, young men
who know that Winnipeg
(200 miles south and not big enough
for a place on the map of the world
in the post office), that Winnipeg
is where the world begins.

THE PEOPLE OF LANSDOWNE

The people of Lansdowne have their own
problems: they want more street lights,
better roads, a bank, the kind of things that
towns that small have always wanted and when
the old men from north of town talk about
what happened at the old Melinski place, they'll
only listen for a while. For months the store
keepers cried "bad business" when no one local
bought the farm; now they only encourage outsiders
to investigate (for the price is low and the land
good) but no one ever buys.

Smith is the richest farmer in Lansdowne (four
combines and a new house) and only the old men
were surprised the summer he rented the farm
to grow wheat. In August when the crop hailed
out a rumour spread that something might be wrong
with the old Melinski place. By October
everyone's harvest had failed. Farmers began
leaving to find other work; their sons married
and moved away; the price of bread went up
two cents in Lansdowne; a week later, winter.

Now only the old men from north of town
want to stay and die in Lansdowne. One of them
talked to Melinski the morning he shot
himself, his wife, his three sons; this old man
has travelled to the city in the south
and when he claims the fences are no boundaries
for the old Melinski place, the people of Lansdowne
only listen for a while. They have problems of their own.

1) 120 MILES NORTH OF WINNIPEG

My grandfather came here years ago,
family of eight. In the village,
nine miles away, they knew him as
the German and they were suspicious, being
already settled. Later he was
somewhat liked; still later
forgotten. In winter everything
went white as buffalo bones and
the underwear froze on the line
like corpses. Often the youngest
was sick. Still he never thought
of leaving. Spring was always greener
than he'd known and summer had
kid-high grass with sunsets big
as God. The wheat was thick,
the log house chinked and warm.
The little English he spoke
he learned from the thin grey lady
in the one-room school, an hour away
by foot. The oldest could hunt, the youngest
could read. They knew nothing of
the world he'd left, and forgotten,
until 1914 made him an alien and
he left them on the land he'd come to,
120 miles north of Winnipeg.

2) DETENTION CAMP, BRANDON, MANITOBA

On the morning of the fourth day,
two men were missing. Later, brought
back, they talked for a while
of some part of summer they'd seen,
then they were quiet, turned bitter,
even a little crazed: these received
no letters from the outside and spoke now
of nothing they wished to return to.
Bodies at night would moan, asleep
with others somewhere who dreamt
of them. The sunrise on the wall
became a condition, the sunset a way
of counting days. The prisoners carried
these things close to their bodies.
This my grandfather came to know
before leaving.

He did not celebrate his homecoming.
His wife was older, his children
came to him less. Even the sky
was not as blue as he'd remembered,
and the harvest, three-quarters done,
reminded him too often of wasted
time, of war in Europe. Winter
came too quickly that year and
next spring the turning of the earth
held no new surprises.

FATHER

Twice he took me in his hands and shook
me like a sheaf of wheat, the way a dog shakes
a snake, as if he meant to knock out my tongue
and grind it under his heel right there
on the kitchen floor. I never remembered
what he said or the warnings he gave; she
always told me afterwards, when he
had left and I had stopped my crying. I
was eleven that year and for seven more years
I watched his friends laughing and him
with his great hands rising and falling
with every laugh, smashing down on his knees
and making the noise of a tree when it cracks
in winter. Together they drank chokecherry
wine and talked of the dead friends and the
old times when they were young, and because
I never thought of getting old, their
youth was the first I knew of dying.

Sunday before church he would trim
his fingernails with the hunting knife
his East German cousins had sent, the same
knife he used for castrating pigs and
skinning deer: things that had nothing
to do with Sunday. Communion once
a month, a shave every third day, a
good chew of snuff, these were the things
that helped a man to stand in the sun for
eight hours a day, to sweat through each
cold hail storm without a word, to freeze
fingers and feet to cut wood in winter, to do

the work that bent his back a little more
each day down toward the ground.

Last Christmas, for the first time, he
gave presents, unwrapped and bought
with pension money. He drinks mostly coffee
now, sleeping late and shaving every day.
Even the hands have changed: white, soft,
unused hands. Still he seems content
to be this old, to be sleeping in the middle
of the afternoon with his mouth open as if there
is no further need for secrets, as if he is
no longer afraid to call his children fools
for finding different answers, different lives.

A WIFE'S FAMILY ALBUM, nearing
the tenth anniversary of her father's death

This, then, is your past; these pictures
the shape of your world before me . . .

The old woman in the flowered dress holds
the child. Her left arm crooks properly;
she has held many children this way, her face
bending toward the child, the smile half-hidden.
The mouth of the child is open, its eyes
closed: it might be crying. Twenty-three years later
the child has become you and you have become
my wife. Soon our picture will be here.

This is the merging of families:
the selective merging of lives. You and I
and our naked undeniable part in this incessant
regeneration of bodies out of bodies. Together
we are melted down for another picture in
the family album: the child will stand like
you stand here, age five, knees and legs fat
and wide apart, your hair yellow, your hat
falling. Behind you, the proud father . . .

Forty percent are dead. Of that, half
are remembered. No one claims to have known
this scowling man we mistook for Disraeli,
greatgrandfather and beginning. On this page, another

cameo to pass by. Then dozens of you, the firstborn,
and him, standing together, your mother watching.

My turn now. They press me between the school
photos and the scenery. The new husband,
son-in-law, brother, friend. Somewhere, further back,
like memos for the future, the yellow pictures of
forgotten friends, the dead father . . .

POEM (for Marge)

Times are when we're
no longer sure of the things
we wanted to say, guessing at least
that we have nothing important
left to report. My father for one
could tell us nothing about cities
yet he knows muskeg and wheat and certain
kinds of weather better than most men
with a daughter and three sons. And
this kind of knowledge, his kind,
is obsolete. And you, for example,
given over to whimsy and occasionally
vodka, you could scarcely say anything
that others would be willing to stop
their life's work and listen to;
still, we spend whole days in conversation
and nothing else.

These are isolated cases. Sometimes
on the subway, about six, after
the executives and secretaries
have gone, I have seen others with
their lunch pails, plaid shirts,
green pants. Construction workers,
brown and mythical, but tough with two
legs apart and braced and sweating.
Perhaps they could tell us something
of value about hard hats, or digging
in the earth: certain of little else
but that and heat. And there have been
children asking for other children in doorways
filled with adults, with more purposes

than playing, with more reasons than
sandboxes and skipping ropes lying
in the sun like snakes. These children,
it's true, disappear quickly.

I have been avoiding the issue, since
things necessarily return to me
and hang about at a safe distance
where they sit on my reason
and demand explanation.

I AM NOT READY FOR THIS MORNING

My life fragments too easily, things
have no core, break up, sometimes end.
I am not tough. The last job
I thought was the right job and now
everything is shaped differently. I write
fewer letters home since I have less to say
that they might want to hear. I spend less
time outside; there is too much risk in
what might happen. My friends have begun
to annoy me in the strangest ways. Yesterday
I yelled at my wife for reading in the dark.
The heads of trees surround me.

In the morning, I am first out of bed, trying
to break into the new day like an advertisement,
pretending the whole day will be fine. The weather
from the bathroom window is halfway to spring
reminding me of pussywillows on the prairies,
or kids in puddles, even the smell of doghair
wet from ozone spring rain. The street
outside is emptying itself onto the next
street, vomiting up its cars, its pedestrians,
its dogs. Only the cats cross diagonally, following
other cats under rotting porch steps where they
howl and fight to make love. I am not ready
for this morning: my face is dry, my hands are dry,
I have spent the night in a desert. Already
I am tired and my body smells of itself.

Every morning I give her my special
kiss and hope that makes some kind of difference.
We kiss cautiously, each holding our

breath back somewhere in our lungs, knowing
it stinks. She sits across the cereal and coffee
from me, looking vulnerable as hell —
about as strong as eggshells — and I start off
saying something nice but my voice is dry
and sounds odd, like a parrot. Meanwhile the black
squirrel sits outside the window, wanting food,
begging the people in the next apartment for peanuts
not bread crumbs. She watches him. This makes
a difference: she crosses her legs, pulls the sash
tight around her waist, and tries the coffee.

I am beginning to understand mornings, the routines,
the failures. After she leaves and I
start waiting for the paper and the want ads, there
is nothing to do. I keep remembering things
that should be done: the dishes, the letters,
everything that hasn't yet been done. The phone
rings once and someone tries to sell me a
computer or a magazine subscription. She phones
to ask about tonight. Am I free? An hour later
I put down my books and go out to the street.
There is no one there. I am trying to understand
whether I am at a beginning or an end. Tonight
I will lay the fragments of the day at her feet
and she will answer for me, she will give me core.

QUEEN STREET TROLLEY

We form jagged rows of bodies and stand now
like a defeated army, with umbrellas, newspapers
and feet as weapons. No one is talking: the trolley
makes all the noise. We have read
and re-read all the ads. We know the shops
by heart, landmarks to count off time: Rubinoff's,
Shumsky's Jewellers, the Public Exchange Mart or
Eaton's with the display window that changes
twice a week and is never twice the same.

There are nearly fifty people here, all
uncomfortable, none familiar or recognized.
The driver continues to insist there is plenty
of room somewhere at the back. Outside the cars
glide by like brilliantly coloured birds while we
move from stop to stop like something wounded.
I am an unknown Lenin nearing Moscow, full of
secret plans for change that are half-forgotten
the moment I am out and walking home.

In the house we are surrounded by nothing more
offensive than tv guides and want ads. We have washed
our hands and prepared for the supper that is
a slow ritual of withdrawal. Here it becomes
safe to dream of quitting work two hours early,
walking out, shouting slogans as we leave. Soon
the laughter begins to come more quickly: the things
that move are moved by us. Control returns.

Yet the heaviness remains. We cannot forget
the timeless clock-watching work, bordered morning
and night by the push and smell of bodies. Already

the morning is in sight. We are not yet asleep
when the journey begins again, full of the
stony senselessness that changes nothing, choked with
a thousand small and nasty turns. Each day
is the same and brings us one day closer to the
angry ideology of random targets and stones.

CHRISTMAS, THE SEASON OF THE TREE

It is a cold night for wonder,
and there is no warmth in the lights.
Our prayers catch in our throats, there is
not one star but many and we cling to our friends
and calculate the dark hours till spring,
now that the grey cold of winter
has arrived and the daylight is so shallow
we catch our breath when it comes as if
we have never seen it before. Soon
the shadows will claim us. Soon we will
fall into the fruitless light of the moon
that covers the earth as bright as snow.

But now we celebrate, if we have not
forgotten how, those of us who have seen
a friend or neighbour die and still manage ourselves
to reason, we celebrate. It must be done
now or not at all. We have heard
the ageless carols and we repeat them
in our dreams for one another and ourselves.
In seven days, it will be
altogether different, a new year, the
possibilities are endless although we recognize
we are no longer children and have learned too easily
to stop. Yet we celebrate
and listen in the night for something
that will make us start again.

In the streets we hurry and we
wonder when the cold will lift. The people
in the shops are eager for the day to end, the
magic hour approaches. We toast each other's

.

health, open the bright gifts
and come back slowly to routine. We have
missed something again, it has gone out of us
and found a better home inside our children.
The cold has trapped us. No one is aware
that outside, on the side of a mountain
where no one lives, a tree
begins to burn.

DREAM

We have travelled and come
to a clearing, a space
that frees us. The trees fold back
and the sun that dances at our feet

has a secret, it can
jerk the sweet peas
from the ground. It is the secret
that pushes birds with half-formed wings
out of nests and into the mouths
of foxes. No one is alarmed. We begin to dance.

We take off our dusty clothes
and lie down in the bright feathers
of new birds. We squat and watch the deer drinking
at the soft edges of the river. We run them
down, pull their great heads
level with the moss, re-discover the strength
of well-placed hands.

Where we bathe the water turns
warm. Nowhere has this happened before.
No one can remember anything as important
as this. Our memories disappear backwards, leave us
alone in this country and unafraid.

We are watching
the willow trees for the first of the diamond-chip
leaves. They come out like hands.
The drink we make from them
fires the mind. We are surely a new breed, men

with sunstroked skin and hands as fast as fish.
We will make this space a

world, we
who have felt the earth as the wolf
has felt it, we

who are the children of the sun.

THE ARRIVAL

1.

Thursday was the first day.
The breakfast noises I knew
never came. No one was home.
All I found was a door left open
and a cup of coffee still hot
and puffing a little grey steam.
Someone had left in a hurry.
Outside was like the house, nothing
moved, no cars ran, no people
walked, only now and then a dog,
nose and tail down at the ground,
crossed a street. I screamed
and everything echoed.
The city stood empty, the city
stood quiet, something had arrived.
Friday there was a new smell
and the sun looked grey. Radio
and telephone buzz-hummed dead.
Saturday the hydro and water went.
I ate the last things and
went behind the house. Sunday
I did it from the steps.
Candles kept me alive — I broke
open stores and cut through the silence to
food. Dogs fought outside every day,
their howls were welcome.
They were wide-eyed now
and once I saw one fall hungry
through a manhole. I carried
a knife. Walked to the lake for water

past the railway station, empty
with trains waiting and rusting.
Airplane overhead, heading south.
I watched. I didn't wave.

2.

Weeks later the buildings went,
the tallest and the churches first.
Each dawn there was a grumble
and one more would come down,
bricks and glass shooting up.
The little houses went with them.
I lost my watch and killed
my first dog, and learned
to sleep in a manhole. Rain
came washing the flat desert
of cement sand and glass sand
down to grey rivers. It rained
for weeks — it was cold.
I was naked, my clothes gone
with the last of the buildings.
I wore a knife in my hand.
Other things started to grow,
grey and plantlike, leaves like
windows, and stems like elevators,
with branches twisted up like streets
running along a river. They grew
tall and glowed at night. The first one
I touched made a noise and I
ran, my hand was bleeding. My dog
has new ones twice over

crawling at her belly. It
snarls at me and watches in the dark
for cats grown suddenly tall. I am
looking for someone remembered as
Eve — the sound of Cain
comes on the wind. There are
white bones at my feet.

3.

The rains have come and gone
as many as my dogs. I am
dying, repeating an unknown word
and marvelling at the shiny thing
in my hand that kills — it had
a special name. Above my head
something crouches and watches
from yellow eyes, springs
down on two curved legs, and walks
upright toward my screaming body.

DOWNTOWN

They stand bare-headed in the stinking rain,
the old men on Parliament Street, talking
about cops and never getting past the uniforms or
the yellow cars with the slogan "to serve and
protect"; sometimes they mention the
plainclothes men because they're harder
to spot, but only from a distance. They'll tell you
they fought at Dieppe or Sicily, one of a generation
who sat by radios all over the world and shook
to the sound of Hitler's voice. They ask where
you're from because they've been there, crossing
the country as many as three times, "looking for,
oh, things . . . " The lucky ones have found
rooms and they sit looking out the windows, red elbows
on the sill, and watch the taxis go by in the rain.
Others have sat on curbs for days, eaten
dogfood, dreamt last dreams; they begged
dimes for coffee and wondered where they'd find a bed
the night other men walked on the moon.

Across the city, there is a different man:
clean-shaven, well-dressed and full of the knowledge
of what he can do. For fifteen years, he has watched
the stock market rise and fall, learning to zero in
on Bethlehem Steel and International Plastics at
precisely the right moment. His company has moved
to a bigger building where the offices are larger,
the desks shine and there are interesting abstracts
on each wall. From his window, he can see
city hall and sometimes when the smog lifts,
the lake. Fourteen men work directly under him;
two women handle payroll and complaints and when

he dines with them, they make jokes about Women's Lib
and hippies. In a fashionable suburb, a wife
waits supper while he moves toward home on
one choked expressway or another, past the factories
where old women put labels on cans or pull levers
eight and a half hours every day. This man has money
and when he goes out at night, he goes to Yonge Street
where the white-hot wickedness of acid rock and
the slow drug-like moving of young bodies disturb him
for as long as it takes to get back to the office
next morning, downtown in the thunderous city.

Every day we drive through this city, like
tourists who have driven far out of their way and
spent the last of their money to find this place
holds nothing delightful. Our friends tell us
America has crossed the border years ago, that the signs
are everywhere: in schools and cities and business,
in the corporate plastic of a Mac's Milk sign.
Their indignation has the edge of a razor sharpened
on the bayonets of National Guardsmen and policemen
throughout the world, their days full of books
by Marcuse or Marx: required preparation for the
celebrated uprising that will lead them forever
out of the hands of the odious strong.

POEM FOR A YEAR AGO
on the death of Pierre Laporte

A year ago, we boarded the bus for Montreal,
left behind the downtown apartment
and felt safe. We sat across the aisle from each other
till Kingston. From then on it rained
and we talked of things that matched the
night and the colourless blur of lights.
Around us passengers smoked or hushed children
and everyone except the driver and those
who sat beside strangers made plans for sleep.

That night the students rioted while we
watched television, refusing to go over again
the arguments on revolution and oppression,
minority rights and the FLQ. Our plan had been
to leave these behind in the downtown apartment,
if not there, then somewhere on the bus. There
was no preparation for the sound from the street
that left us naked in our clothes, that left no space
for good sounds coming out of the past: the nights
of driving fast over loose gravel roads somewhere
in the back country where the cops can't find you,
your belly tight with beer, your ears ringing
with the noise of a couple struggling
in the backseat. And the music, at full volume,
telling you to be young or wild or both.

Our journeys have become shorter, away
from cities, up toward Land's End or Christian Island
where the big newspapers are sometimes a day late.
Here we can forget those grand plans we made
from small safe places a year ago, before

we ran and thought by running
to escape. Now we want to freeze everything.
The bird in flight. The touching of hands.
The sniper's bullet the moment it breaks
the warm reluctant skin . . .

October 17, 1970

THE MAGIC MEN

The magic men
have gone, the last one
beats against my plans with a handshake
and disappears.

The last one wears a grey suit
that makes him disappear from time to time
in the middle of crowds. Now
he enters my dreams, touches my body like hair,
and turns his life toward me like a watch.
His eyes and hands are saying *You are like me*
when I was young; you must understand
the way I am now, my life of moving,
the nights of alcohol and long walks. Understand
you have no choice.

    (In Alberta I am a boy, so small
    that I look up in my dreams
    to see the faces of men. Their shoulders

    are wider than my father's. Up here
    I see the brown ponies running like water
    west to the blue mountains. This one teaches me

    to ride a bareback horse, his hands
    hold me safe, the mare walks
    between my legs, rubs the loins

    toward a quick first life.)

The last man is not a public man. No one
can imagine his life at home: whether he uses

aspirin, if he likes music, the status
of his wife. No one
needs to know. In his eyes across the table
I find myself. In the grey smile I could rest
or be lost forever. This is the hero
I meet over cigarettes and beer
while the party swirls upward and away, one
of the wordless magic men. *You must understand*
the way I am now; you are like me
when I was young . . .

    (The brother who is most like my father,
    the brother who is always tall, he
    understands guns and what it means

    to hunt and wait and kill. The birds
    come closer. Warning me again
    not to move, he rises with the gun

    as one thing, firing as a machine
    would fire. It is enough
    to find the dead and watch him, his eyes

    full of the sky and quiet gun.)

Now the heroes have become older
as if they understand what they do
best, and that it can best be done
quietly. These are the men who will move
outward and fail, finding the same things
others recognize in backyards
and empty beds. The magic men

are leaving: *Come with us,*
we have waited long enough, you have
no choice. Come with us, we have waited
long enough . . .

JOURNEY INTO WINTER

1.

Her hair badly out of place, she sleeps
beside me as I sit watching the dark outside
our window grow more familiar than the train
and occasionally when she moves a little, she
wakes enough to reach out and touch me and know
that I am still there. No one gets off here.
North Shore Hotel, four lights and a snowed-in
car; the horn sounds, we move on. The woman
in the next seat begins to snore and I remember
again that I am going home . . . Marathon
(there is a picture of Lake Louise in the
waiting room, a Norman Rockwell calendar
from Ray's Service in the men's) is half-way
there. Here she meets the first of my family
and is suddenly afraid to talk, holding my arm
so tightly that I know I have already begun
to change . . . We run away to the beach and
the egg-smooth stones to be alone, talking
right up to the Indian graveyard we didn't know
was there and thinking, "This must last!" It
took another twelve hours to make Winnipeg.

2.

And suddenly stuck again in the patterns
of my friends' imaginings: violent, moody,
sensitive, concerned, crude, I grow restless,
annoyed with Winnipeg for never changing for us,
for anyone returning: still flat, still old,
still overproud. We've used that up,
consumed it till only the decay of memories

remains, surrounding us like the cold . . . Together
we walk places we walked alone before,
before meeting in T.O. and deciding suddenly one
night in a laundromat that we could love. The places
are not the same: Memorial Park and the snow
does not lie like the blanket I remember; it
clings to the ground, covers buildings, suffocates
the earth . . . We meet each other's old
friends and she becomes my explanation for
having changed and I am hers. Three days later
we leave for the farm; old memories rise to meet us.

3.

The changes I saw I knew were my own, not
theirs. Only my mother's arthritis
is real; the hand bent slightly to the side
and swollen to stiffness, each movement
full of the slow pain that leaves half her duties
to strangers . . . Now the daughters-
in-law are washing the dishes; others pick up
the collage of paper ripped from presents resting
now under the tree, a green flame by the window;
I carry water from the well outside and begin again
those things I have always done, falling back
into the stillness of adult sons at home and
having only half my energies to meet my mother's
questions in that one sharp inevitable moment
at the kitchen table . . . Then leaving,
past the town (32 Christmas cards specially
priced for a dollar), out of the country where
farmers vote conservative every time and green

is seven colours in the summer, out of the winter
where it will be two months till someone thinks
to say the days are getting longer (mornings
are dark till ten and every man wonders if this day
will cloud), we are leaving this again and only
by tomorrow will we be part of a landscape we can bear
to watch: the white and nameless snow, the movement
of trains, the never-ending line of tracks . . .

A HOUSE IN THE COUNTRY

Driving up to the house, the rain
on the windshield as big as cat tracks,
we divided the house into theirs and
ours. At the gate we said again
it was a good house, that we would all
have good times here. Later in the kitchen
we counted our money and slept, content
for a while to be done with business . . .

Later still, we would quarrel and leave
each other a new kind of silence. Standing
alone in the blue parlour, I discover the
house: the earth, red and fine, resting
on the windows; the yellow pine floors;
the knowledge that others have lived here:
this, perhaps, has something to do with love.
Or nothing, like the plants outside, white
with the light of the room and moving toward
the glass as if straining to see this new
intruder who stands alone in the middle
of his thoughts, at the periphery
of another blind allegiance . . .

Against mine, the curve of her back
reminds me of the unchanging things. Upstairs
the laughter of friends. Then silence,
and the desperation to remember beginnings,
haunted by the sound of all our first things.

LETTER FOR A FRIEND

"When you look at a piece of delicately spun glass you think of two things: how beautiful it is and how easily it can be broken."
—from *The Glass Menagerie* by Tennessee Williams

1.

If our world is glass, it is
neither beautiful nor easily broken. The walls
of our wine bottle are thick with
nearly thirty years of living. And we are getting older.
For six months of weekends we drank enough
to get up to the edge and kept drinking
to stay there. For six months
we made glass walls stand as strong as stone. Inside,
watching half-heartedly for cracks, we built
small fires and invited
friends only.

You left before I did, needing more space
than I had ever wanted. You sent letters back
explaining from time to time
that I shouldn't be afraid to follow. You had found
both love and work and I could do the same.
I burned everything, melting
the glass into a small ball that I swallowed
without water: you have built
a wall around my guts.

Now we approach things in the same way
only because we approach them. Everything else
is different. I am forgetting how
to understand you and you

are ahead of me, building places anyone
can enter. I have seen them
and they are warm but dangerous. You are admired
from many places and many people
tell me your work with others is endless. Still,
I feel that I am waiting for you. When you return
my applause will deafen
everyone.

2.

And our friends are getting older, Don,
as we are. Your kids are almost old enough
to be the new generation: they will
push us out.

And what happens here and now
passes like the sunlight and the rain
while we eat and talk and make do
as if nothing could change. And what has passed
leaves nothing that we could take
in one hand and break or shape into something
round or warm. Only a small scar
appears and circles a major vessel running out
from the heart. Yesterday is someone else's
day. It belongs to one of the thousand
babies born then. It belongs to
retrospect and calendars
and madness.

I sleep now with my arms tight against my chest
to protect the pain that starts there

and wakes me. I have seen you in the morning
vomiting in the washroom. I have wanted
to ask where do we go today. You
would have an answer although you are
as uncharted in your life as I am
in mine. You are waited for outside your house.
Someone has been counting on you for years.
Like homing pigeons they will
find you, they will make
nests inside you for their angry young.
And they will leave you nothing but filth and small worms.
And a scar the size of a bull's eye
or a moon.

This could happen tomorrow. This,
or something worse. All our words then
will be as useless as human
shit. All our loving will be nothing but
footnotes to a nightmare. And everything
will go on like clockwork with all the clocks
spinning back.

3.

I have seen you looking for yourself
in women throughout the city. You said
each one of them could offer you something
you had probably lost. Their hands
were rubber bands they tied around your head
to pull you closer. You offered them
wine and gave them good
times, calculating each move to cut

all connections. You claimed superiority
and mashed them like flowers when they won.
Someday you will enter your dream and find
an arena full of women waiting
to take you. You will be laughing,
alone in the crowd and the musk,
and laughing.

But you have settled outside your dream.
With one woman, you mix raw energy and anger
and demand that she remember the time
you lived alone. Both of you
have lived at the very edges of your bodies
for a year. If the blood has not yet changed
to wine, the odour of blood
has gone. You are certain only
of warmth, only that it flows.

4.

Don, you will drive us all
crazy. You tell us about the day
you drank yourself blind in Kingston and got
thrown into jail, how the guards took
your money and your belt and didn't believe
a word about you being an important professor
at the universiy, you tell us each detail as if
it had happened to someone else, a close friend perhaps
or someone you knew for a short time
five years ago. You make us stretch until
we fit none of the things
we once were. You make us laugh

until our minds bleed like
old medieval wounds.

Your friends explode questions
around your head while you move back and
forth among them like a hungry
half-mad dog. You understand they need
you. You understand they have made you
a hero. Beyond them, there is
an empty plain of waste and white buildings.
They form walls around you, walls
that come toward you, come at you. I will
be a wall that stands without moving. I
will be a glass wall. See through me —
then take me down.

ACROSS CANADA, WEST FROM TORONTO

Before Winnipeg, only the familiar well-travelled
roads, weaving in and out of the ageless
evergreen bush . . .

Across the top of Saskatchewan we ate
Sweet Marie chocolate bars and counted
everything that moved: the new birds, the
hitchhikers, gophers. We formed alliances
with the car ahead and the car behind,
travelling this way for fifty miles, like
partners in a dance. Ahead of us, a country
forever too large for one man's mind; behind us,
more of the same.

Edmonton looked like Winnipeg, and
Winnipeg had looked like something else . . .

Moving west, the world rises and the horizon
peaks, a mile above the timberline. We roar
through rock cuts between valleys, across valleys
filled with mist and swollen rivers, places
pioneers never went or went at twenty miles a day.
Split Peak, Wild Horse Lake, Glacier: names
for the untamed and places enough to convince you
these mountains will never change, that of all things
they have come the closest to lasting forever.

There is so much road behind us; there is
always more ahead: these are the facts of a continent.
We stop for a moment, beside this road
the length of the country, to check our maps,
and then move on, dreaming of the Pacific.

LAMENT FOR FRIENDS EXPECTED AT CHRISTMAS

Now in the night, knowing
you will not be here to make me laugh,
the thought of your absence does not
go to sleep nor does it help to go back
slowly through the day remembering the moments
when I might have started easily enough
without you: a cat chasing the shadows of
winter birds that feed on the apples
we left behind, or the long sound of trains
that call out of me all that I have.
There is no beginning, only
the January sun hanging like
diamonds on the snow and the trees that run
naked as veins across the sky.

Yet there are good things this season
has shared with me: I have made
more friends and the old friends have not yet
left me behind. And only friends
can protect me from this land where the snow
does not melt, where we must all
make room for it inside ourselves. We have made
a brotherhood that works, a pact that remembers
how the last day of the year was brilliant,
how the sun hung about our house all day.

But now it is quiet and the night
is full of things I cannot move: it is
no longer possible to leave and
take the best things with me. It would be better
if you were here, if there was laughter,
or an explanation for winter that would

break it. But there is nothing, only night, only
the sound of trains rolling over snow
in your direction, beating
like great hearts that groan and move
out across the country and the space
between us that is the last cold distance
till summer.

TRAVELLING THE INDIAN COUNTRY

1.

The runners of the Magpie leave
an hour before sunrise and are expected to return
when the moon reaches the lip
of the great river. They are expected
to bring

good news of the falling water and the river
mist. On their way they will pass
the landmarks the chief spoke of: a bend in the river
that is like the hind leg of a running wolf,
a lake they must cross that is
without bottom, a stand of tamaracks so thick the sun
cannot touch the ground.

The runners will avoid the open spaces
where the Cree will be camping. They will know the Cree
by the smell of their horses which is the smell
of the Cree and their women. The Magpie will run

until the first sight of the cliffs. Then
they will stop and wait for the mist
to show them it is safe

to go on. They will remember the Magpie princess
who died near this spot when the mist
was not favourable. And they will wait.

If the runners do not return when the moon
touches the lip of the white river,
the chief will know
the Magpie can go no further, he

will know the runners were not the bravest among them

as the mist will have known. He will
lead the women and the children back
to the waterless forest and not try again that season

to reach the mist. His warriors will hide themselves
from the Cree and keep away
from the women. A child born in this season
must be left by the river. The runners know this,

know what happens when they fail.

2.

For two days we have tried
to drive out of the rainy weather. This morning
we were certain two hundred miles would

give us the sun. Instead
we are six hours on the road and coughing
from the rain. Someone in the backseat

is crying. This is not how any of us
expected the country to be, this place
where the wind is like a gunshot against the car,
coming up from the water like a demon,
rocking us back and forth between the white lines
and the trees. If we were warm

and certain of each other, we
could be laughing at this crazy land. Instead we are

six hours on the road and riding
the small silences that
keep us apart, that make us

avoid what we are and what we leave unsaid.
Who will cook, who will drive, how far,
how fast, where to stop, where to stay, the chance
of reaching Indian Falls before dark:

these are the questions we throw around
like arrows. For the time that's left
we turn toward the road maps on our knees
and watch the thin red lines we crawl along, each of us

aimed for the point where
the road will end and give us back our private
possibilities. For the time that's left, we sit alone

with the world outside out windows
full of rain and we listen to the wind

and we watch for better weather up ahead.

3.

In the space a hundred
feet above the falls, the Magpie chief stands.
Behind him the runners, then the tribe.
Along the cliffs, trees cling together

like the fingers of old men. There is nothing
in front of him but the mist

47

and the empty space that ends at the bottom
of the falls, the home

of the river god. Here

there is no sound but the sound of water
as it falls one hundred feet, two
hundred feet and turns yellow foam to blue-white-

rising-up-like-smoke mist. One
by one the warriors come forward and lean down to wet
their right arms in the dusty water: this

will give more strength
than the heart of a wolverine, it will
make the hunt easier, make certain the victory
over the Cree and the new enemies

who come out of the rising sun, who must be met
before the first snow, these enemies
no Magpie understands and who carry

no arrows a Magpie can see.

4.

Everywhere the water

is like an animal. It feeds along the rock shore
where we stand, reaches as high
as the first birch

and falls back into the yellow river water.
We shout back and forth, take
pictures to send somewhere else, stand around. This energy

that shakes the ground under our feet
cannot be measured. We cannot believe it continues
when we are not there. We must

do something to be
counted. Our sticks and pieces of rock
disappear without

a sound. We find separate paths
and follow them along the river, none far enough
to get beyond the sound

of falling water, white falling
water that none of us will change. We acknowledge
this strength and we are

afraid of it. The night is coming and we prepare to sleep
while the loons cry out

to each other, or to
themselves and what they say

mixes with our dreaming.

5.

Where the moss drapes across the stones

like the hide of a furry animal and the lichens
are sequins that end

where the water begins, the Magpie sit
and know that waiting is not enough: the mist
will rise no higher, cover no more Magpie land,
make the warriors no fiercer.
The mist demands amulets

and the best made arrows. The river requires
the horns of the fastest deer and the heart
of a mad black bear. At dawn of the second day

the Magpie will give up their best things
to the water. All day
they will wait and when the sun is gone
they will watch the strongest brave leap

and curve as he leaps, watch

as he drops like a stone through the rainbow
and strikes the bottom of the falls

without a sound.

They will follow his body
past the rapids where three women
will swim out and tie the brave in their hair.
On the shore the chief will mark
the body into sections with the end of a
burnt stick and the women will

burn the heart, bury

the rest. Then the mist will rise
higher. The Magpie will return to their forests,
ready for the enemy. And when it rains

the women will have no difficulty coaxing warriors
into their tents. They will tell
their lovers the falling rain

is the kiss of the river god.

6.

We are six, not
a tribe but a caravan of chance. Tonight

we talked and discovered
we were still alone. Perhaps the weather
will be better tomorrow. Perhaps

we will agree to stop beside some river
where we might fish or sit across the water
away from each other

for a while. Or we might drive on, knowing
we cannot get back to what we wanted
when we began. By noon
we will have gone a hundred miles and someone

will want to go a hundred more

before dark. We will hurry for an hour
and then remember how we hurried to make

Indian Falls, and arrived
to find we could not be welcomed. Tonight
the shadows have reached back and touched us
and for a moment the rain and the wind

didn't count, but
it was never enough: there are things
we cannot give up, not

here, not now. Tomorrow there will be

no new efforts and we will go slowly
and watch the things we pass. We will pitch
our tents and make our separate fires, and will have

nothing much to say. All around us
the wind will sound like falling water, the tents
and the cars will vanish in the coming
of the night, and we will sleep through dreams

of a land without distance,
land without rain.

THE MOUNTAINS HAVE NOT YET ENTERED

The mountains have not yet entered
my dreams and become familiar as the cities
and the old places where the land
is flat and the shadows are my own.
The mountains will come, their high grey
iguana fringe of peaks will come
broken and shoved up into the snow and ice.
They will come as the violent cities
came, as the flat land came and went.

There will be no struggle with these
mountains. It is best to go as high as
the loggers' road, above the valley
where the air is cold and thin forever.
If this place does not warm and feed you it will
warm and feed no others. You will find
other ways to survive. Those who come after you
riding in from the world will find only
your camp fires, left from the time
when only fire made you warm.

The daylight blue of these mountains
will heal you, the white of their snow
will mark each day a new beginning.
You will recognize as yours the land as high
as the timberline, the yellow tamaracks
and the soft green pines that wrap around
the shoulders of the mountain. And above that,
that is your land too, above everything
in the fusion of rock with rock.
Your boundaries start at the river
and end in the yellow sun, hanging there,

where you reach it from the snow.

It is a safe place to live. At first
the dark will make you cry out, you will be
eager for faces. That will pass.
Eventually the night air will surround you
like the breath of God. When the end comes
you will not be thinking of it.
The river will carry your bones out of the valley
down to the people and the houses of light.
They will be used as driftwood — that is
as it should be: you cannot live here
if you do not change.

It will be years before they discover the space
you lived in. They will come after you
with their equipment and their maps.
They will trace back and find
the trails of other men, and above that
they will find your place, the
strange markings and the hollow rocks.
They will spend the winter here but they
will not survive. Only the child will stay.
He alone has seen your flesh bind together
the mountains as easily as ice. In time
he will enter your world. Then there will be
two of you. The mountains will enter
a long and pleasant spring.

CYCLES, for Marge

We have not left the old pain
behind, we have merely
found inside it a clearing that is calm,
a space such as this valley where the trees
reach up like hands for the light
and the mountains make a bowl for the sun.
Even here the liberties are taken and the normative
uncertainties keep pace and surface
in our dreams and in our
failures with friends and one another, even here
there is still the sonorous waiting
between us: we will probably not die
together, nor at the same time, yet the sound of crying
stays inside like
blood itself, or fear.

Yet if you are right we will have a
compassionate destiny outside
the flow of circumstances, then we can
lie down like the fingers of the same hand
remembering how far we have come from
the beginnings in Winnipeg in
Toronto, groping out of the ego
and every day our needs shifting under our feet like
sand. And nothing was taken
that had not been given and nothing was assumed
not the giving nor the desire not even
the future though it formed around us anyway
and from the first trembled like water
in our hands.

This is a new geography, a sheltered

valley like the soft world inside a
fist and although it is flawed by the men around us
who slide as easily as seasons through
their lives and although it is broken
by our own anxieties and our need for friends, it is
still familiar: we have been here
before and we did not expect to find it
here but we have been here before. Three years
have passed, turning like miles and like
only once before, we are together.

BEAUTIFUL WOMAN

1.

Beautiful woman, you crown the hours
and we grow wonderful, we grow secret
in the assumption of our life. How easily
the electric night warms us. Fish
swim past the edges of our bed, oceans
in their mouths. The morning will never come
and break down this fever to be mad in each other's
warm white skin. We go down
like children, we go down into a great moaning
with silence forgotten and floating through the ceiling
like balloons. See me, see me dancing
to your terrible music, woman. The room
is filling with candles, the sun
is inches away: it smells
of your hair and lies writhing in your palm.
See again the sun and the bed wet with warm rain.
Wave after wave it comes, wave
after wave stones
break open at our touch, small bones break free and drift
out of you into me. And the skin
becomes water and salt shuddering
out past fingers — bloodfilled and animal —
towards the centre
of a thick and velvet earth where the sun
burns a hole in the sky.

2.

Yet even from this bed
the anger rises day by day
and digs trenches to fortify its seed. So we

swear, accuse, sometimes punch flat-handed
the stubborn skin. You tell me
what it means to wait and work afternoons
with dishes and floors. You tell me
my friends who pace and strut ignore you, or notice
only your sex. How you hate them!
See your tears fly out at them like diamond-headed
spikes. See that it's me you've hit.
Let that sound surround our bed, let it
fill up the room as high as the windows.
Put your hungriest cats to prowl inside my skin.
Let nothing escape: the mouth
will stretch and harden into my best smile.
(You know this is not like a movie, you know
this is not in our dream — yet it continues.)
Everywhere muscles are dying. Out of my throat
you will hear me cursing, you will hear me
roaring. When it is my turn
nothing will change. The mirror
will fall, history will vomit at your name.

3.

It is morning and the yellow sun falls
through the window like a stone. In the kitchen
the dishes wait and bits of swollen meat
have stuck to the sides of knives. All around us
broken flesh is aching. Tonight
we will go deep into our powerful
bodies again. Or we will do nothing
and survive just the same. Woman,
wake up and hold me, I have

nowhere else to take my anger. Wake up and let
your hands spread like warmth along my back.
Now that the skin is dead. Now
that both the music and the bruises have gone.
And all that remains refuses to begin
without falling, is
caught and held in the light that spills
off the floor and stains the bed
like wine.

SICKBED

The bed revolves, smells, I am useless out of it.
The hearts at the end of each finger beat
separately, out of time with each other, as birds
in a cage. Only sleep can take me
where I want to go, not here, this sudden
coldness and the heat that goes out of you in waves until you
drift. The evening and the night
move by at their leisure, in full bloom.
The dark jells, the clock replaces the sun.
My death will come at night: I know that now.
I have carried it that long,
it is like the feather of a dark bird: at night
it wants to fly.

I fall into my dream and the direction of my blood
is like a silver pipeline.
My muscles flex and plunge.
There is something in me like water, it
reaches out for sand, for air, trees, birds,
unlimited sky: I remember
what it feels like, the earth under foot,
not merely this square of window or the light
dropping like a shadow through the door. You take
all you can, the fall wind that touches your cheek
gives you winter, your eyes
burn toward the future. You are standing
half-way up a hill — the cool wind
slips in and out of your shirt — getting ready
to run for the lake and the sun
like a boy.

The room is cold and there is a wetness

at the edges of the bed.
It is time to try again, to open the windows
and speak to this simple dawn without the words
breaking sideways in the round
foulness of my mouth. Already the dream
recedes, the bed pulls you back, your shirt
lies open at the throat while the wind from the hill
drops through the window like a bird
and curls itself in deep, deep
in your breathless side.

LAKE

In the morning, along the vacant shore,
when the water is still cool
and the trees bend down as if to drink,
there is a quietness like the deer who come for water
in the small round seconds of the dawn: the denials
are forgotten, the tough work of balance and
maintenance and hope has not yet begun.
It is a different place now, this view
that is a panorama, that is also
a reflection, these million leaves
opening like mouths to the sun and to the light
that rolls down the mountain, down
to the water in the urgent greeting that
turns the water blue and white and once more
familiar like the beautiful
brown hands of summer.

By evening, even the water does not flow
toward me: there is no order
outside the kind I need to impose and I
step back so easily into
a void at the end of the day where the
calm is waiting and I can
kneel down and let it touch my hands, let it
cool the palms and wash upwards over the shoulders
and the thin blind eyes. Now the lake
is company enough. Later I may turn,
leave the great dark face of the water
and take those first sweet steps
back to the earth.

POEM FOR AN OLDER FRIEND'S
BIRTHDAY, March 31, 1972

My generation has not been kind
to either of us: they have taught me
I am different from you
merely because I am younger; they have told me
you would not understand the way I live
or the things my life must do.
But they were wrong: in your time
you fought against the things
that I am fighting now. Now it is possible
to win and if I could touch these words
and make them sing, they would make
a better kind of praise. But the difficulties of giving
have stopped me a dozen times before.
There is no easy way to understand
the unspoken embarrassment that hangs like a knife
between the honest emotions of men,
or the way well-meaning words run
through the smooth arrangements like a river
through a gorge. Whatever else
is lost, the turbulence remains —

Yet the things we cannot share
are not measured in words or years, they are
counted in moments: I have not been to war,
I have not buried a best friend.
Was it different on your first jump, the airplane
going on without you, your parachute
opening above you like an exclamation mark?
Or later, with the children wanting
what they could not give back.
Or at the linotype when your future

sat down beside you, smelling bad — you made
a new one in two weeks, moving as I have moved,
as I will move again. These thousand differences
that have made us strangers have made us
laugh — we all have our stories,
the hours out of the past that
chase after us, the unfair ceremonies
we have danced to over and over, we learn them again.
But it is not a daily operation, this
remembrance, this jousting: we survive
in our own ways: they are
separate things, beautiful in their own right
and painful as a man's love for a woman
is painful, is right —

If you do not want
this birthday then, if you say each year
binds you closer to your body, that it
makes you older than a man my age,
remember there are those around you
who will notice no difference in the passage
of a day. What they see of you
they would trade for their own lives:
your way of walking as if you mean
never to stop anywhere very long, the pride
you take in work well-done. Remember
you have given me a better future
than any other friend, it will take its place
outside the cliches and the dogmatism.
I will measure my success by yours, I will
face the tangled circumstances and the

unwanted direction, knowing now
even this way there will be
something real. In the first light of the morning
we will fish for it. There is
plenty of time: it will only take a moment,
one bright blue moment and the fish
flashing its haphazard life
in the air —

TARGET PRACTICE AT FINDLAY CREEK

The old cabins along the creek
stopped us, like the 1933 licence plate
and the homesteads on the alkali flats.
The men who panned this creek for gold
when the bright veins at Wild Horse ran out,
where did they finally die
and would they remember their work here
or imagine the way it is now? collapsing, almost
gone, the rot and the rust, the animals
and the trees coming back. And two strangers
crossing their land with guns
looking for targets and a little peace.

It had been five years but the feeling of the gun
was still familiar: the sound
and the surprise against your shoulder.
Neither of us imagined I would shoot
so well. I shot down deer, and grouse
at fifty yards. I shot down the differences
between us. I shot down time.
We were boys again, shooting crows for
ten cents a pair of legs, and squirrels for supper.
We were Findlay Creek men, living only as well
as we hunted, and living well,
each small round hole something wounded
or dead, this time at least
a sign of friendship between men.

When we left the high country,
we passed the sluice boxes and the ditches
one last time and did not reach the valley floor
until the shadows touched across the road.

We were almost home and thinking of
other homes, years back, full of strangers now
but we did not ask what it meant, we drove,
we could not afford to remember much more.
We drove, the rifle on the seat between us,
the smell of gunpowder on our hands, wondering how
long it would take to go all the way back.

WAITING AT EVENING

The sun almost down and the day
settling inside me like sediment, its
terrible movements keep stirring while
in front of me the mountains go
purple, go bright in the sun, the snow
shining like a light. And the evening
in slow and constant change now that I am alone
and waiting for the nighthawks to come, alone
with the robins in the green grass,
the casual movements of horses beyond the fence
where the apple blossoms are falling
like snow or light, the crystal
evening light. And everywhere the day shifts
inside me with its own kind of life and my need
to separate it out, to give it
a sense of its own so it can
leave me.

And still I will inhabit
the bitter geography of my own making, a place
where the roots rise up
and choke me or hold too tightly
when I want most of all to move. And the small
dry bones of friendship, they are here too,
the repeat performance of my failures when I have
stepped out of my heart and out of
my friends' lives in order to survive.
And for them there is still
the greatest need to hurt
again and again
                    and still be loved.
Or at least be held as the light holds me now

folding and bending around me so softly
that for a moment I lose sight of it and know
only the sharp brooding hazards of the day:
it is always this way, what I change
I also destroy. Now I build from
new dreams and some dreams I can't tell anyone.

And still the dark rises,
coming up like an army of the blind, bending
across the fields and the valley, breaking
before my vision like glass. And there, a
jet, moving out of the east like a
carefully drawn chalk line, going up
through a cloud, fanning out, becoming itself
a cloud. It becomes time to go inside
again, there are still
no clues. The nighthawks
have not yet arrived. There are only a few stars.

ON THE TRAIL TO THE TOP OF THE WORLD

On the trail to the top of the world
    the smell of the earth comes,
        clover, water,
        the cracked ground or
        apples turning their hot faces to the
sun, it comes, opening inside you
like the first flower of earth until there is no
world like this one, no sky or trees
    like these although you suspect
        the potential for change
        as you would anticipate
        a storm.

    But you go toward it
        despite the reluctance and the fear
you go toward it any way you can, past
        the tremors and the
        false signposts, there is
a centre that attracts you and you find it
    suddenly: the opening into
        an organized life, a
        world you fit into
perfectly, as water in a river,
        child in the womb.

    And you cannot believe
        it has always been here:
it is all here, the agreements and the
good examples, the company of love, you are
        the child you were
        the old man you will become, it is
earth without end: where you live no matter

where you are, now that you have left the never-ending trail,
    now that you have gone through the last stand
        of words and things
    and seen the beautiful green light at the
    edge of the clearing that is still this country's
        first promise of home.

Anansi Poetry

The Circle Game, *Margaret Atwood*
Power Politics, *Margaret Atwood*
Nobody Owns Th Earth, *bill bissett*
The Gangs of Kosmos, *George Bowering*
Body, *Robert Flanagan*
Incisions, *Robert Flanagan*
Airplane Dreams, *Allan Ginsberg*
The Army Does Not Go Away, *David Knight*
Civil Elegies And Other Poems, *Dennis Lee*
Soundings, *eds. Ludwig and Wainwright*
The Collected Works of Billy
   the Kid, *Michael Ondaatje*
Mindscapes, *ed. Ann Wall*
The Dream Animal, *Charles Wright*
Year of the Quiet Sun, *Ian Young*
I am Watching, *Shirley Gibson*
Crusoe: Poems Selected And New, *Eli Mandel*
Waterloo Express, *Paulette Jiles*
At The Edge of the Chopping There
   Are No Secrets, *John Thompson*
Poems for All the Annettes, *Al Purdy*

7-301